THE GOSPEL FOR CHILDREN

object messages from the Gospel of Mark

HAROLD J. UHL

Augsburg Publishing House
Minneapolis, Minnesota

THE GOSPEL FOR CHILDREN

Copyright © 1975 Augsburg Publishing House

Library of Congress Catalog Card No. 75-14695

International Standard Book No. 0-8066-1493-5

Scripture quotations unless otherwise noted are from the Revised Standard Version of the Bible, copyright 1946, 1952, and 1971 by the Division of Christian Education of the National Council of Churches.

Manufactured in the United States of America

Contents

5

Introduction

A message understood by children is understood by all. Thus the time devoted especially to the younger members of the Christian fellowship is time well spent. It makes the little ones feel that they are a part of the church, and gives them an easily remembered lesson to carry with them. Every child looks forward to that special message. Quite practically, it is a break in what can be a long time for the younger child who attends worship. This is especially true if the children get a chance to leave their seats and walk to a place closer to the pastor. The entire congregation, however, should be able to hear the content of the message.

The adults at a worship service listen as intently as the children to a brief, colorful message. In speaking to the children one can be far more free and lighthearted even in a congregation that prefers formality, for everyone unbends for the sake of children, and enjoys it.

A children's message, therefore, offers a special opportunity to introduce a concept into the service prior to the lessons or the sermon. It provides a warm-up that ties in with the readings or the homily.

Every message in this book is based on the Gospel of Mark and is associated with an object. Sometimes the object is shown and pondered as a way of fixing attention on the speaker or arousing curiosity while introducing the point of the lesson. Sometimes the object is shown only after a few words of introduction. Sometimes, however, the object is something the speaker or children do; play a game, interview a child, or the like. My experience has shown that action enhances interest and rapport.

Besides the constant support of my wife, Barbara, I must acknowledge a few who have been of great help in the preparation of this material:

- Hope Church in Annandale, Virginia, for whom I first prepared children's messages and who have always responded with encouraging appreciation.

- My children, Alison, Evelyn, Brian, and Wayne, who gave me insight as they grew up and who gladly shared toys and pets and things to show at church.

- Emma and Ted Bremer who have provided impetus for writing by their constant interest.

HAROLD J. UHL

Cleaning Up
for Jesus

It will happen in almost every house in the days before Christmas. One day you come home and discover the whole room is moved about. The chairs are away from the wall, the vacuum cleaner is out and mother is dusting and cleaning. Or maybe one Saturday morning you wake up and find everyone is up, sweeping and waxing. You know what's coming, so you wait a bit and, sure enough, one of your parents says, "Now today I want you to clean up your room. All toys have to be put away and we'll sweep the floor so everything will be nice."

"Why?" you say. "Because grandmother is coming," or your aunt, or friends, or somebody is coming for the holidays, "and we want everything to be clean and ready for them."

After all, that's the way to enjoy having visitors, making the house attractive, making them feel welcome, getting

Scripture: Mark 1:1-8

Object: *Housecleaning equipment (broom, mop, dustcloth, etc.)*

---

things ready so you don't have to scurry around doing lots when they arrive—so everything is ready.

This is a time to get ready. Not just for guests, but for God. Jesus is coming into our lives—as we say, "into our hearts." The cleaning we do for Jesus does not use brooms or dustcloths. For Jesus we want to sweep away the things that are wrong in our lives, the things which would not make him feel at home. Maybe it's that we should be helping, or maybe it's that we feel mean about somebody else whom Jesus would like for us to love.

God helps change things like that and he forgives us for ever being that way. He even gives us people (like John the Baptizer) to warn us and help us; parents, friends and teachers.

This is the time for us to get ready by cleaning out all our sins. Get ready. Jesus is coming.

Chosen to Work
with God

Thank you, Jane. I want to ask you something. How did you feel when you were selected out of the group? *(If no response. . . . Were you happy? scared? proud?)* Let's see then, you were selected and then you were given all those good lollypops; you had a job to do. You had to go and make the other girls and boys happy by giving them each a lollypop. You are really someone special.

At the beginning of his Gospel, St. Mark talks about when Jesus was baptized. When that happened he knew he was someone special. He had been selected. He knew he was the Son of God and had lots of good things to do, because he

Scripture: Mark 1:4-11 (especially vv. 9-11)

Object: *Select one child from the group. This can be done by numbered "tickets," a chair previously marked or other chance means (rather than selection by skill or guessing something). Then give the child a basket of lollypops (or wrapped candy) and ask him or her to distribute them to the others, and come back to you.*

---

was given God's Spirit. Baptism picked him out and gave him a job to do.

The wonderful thing is that when we are baptized the same thing happens. God calls us by name and gives us his Spirit. God selects us to be his own, that is, he gives us all the strength and joy and desire to go and do good things for God in our world. Of course, our job isn't the same as Jesus' job. He was to save the whole world. Maybe your job is just making someone happier, but God gives you all you need, whatever you are to do.

Baptism is a wonderful thing. God has picked you out and called you by name so you can go to work with him.

Repentance,
A Tool for Building

A hatchet is a wonderful thing. Some people look at a hatchet and say, "Oh, that's something to cut with," and they think of chopping down trees or clearing things away and getting rid of things. I suppose you could use a hatchet just to cut and destroy things, but if you know a scout, you may know this is a wonderful tool for someone in the woods or the wilderness.

You can cut wood to build a fire to be warm or to cook. A hatchet can shape a peg to keep up a tent, and even hammer the peg into the ground. Or in the wilderness a scout can even use a hatchet to build a shelter to sleep under for the night. Sometimes he might make marks along a trail so others can follow him, or so he can find his way home and not get lost.

Scripture: Mark 1:12-15

Object: *Boy Scout hatchet*

You see, just because it cuts doesn't mean that a hatchet just tears down, instead it helps and builds.

Jesus met the devil in the wilderness, in a lonely place, and triumphed over him. We also have a way to overcome evil in our lives. We are told to repent, to cut out our wrong ways; to change what we're doing. This isn't just to make things hard for us, or just to take away part of our lives, but in order to build a better life. Repenting means chopping away our sins so we can clear a place for God. It is like marking a new trail so we can find our way back to God.

Like a hatchet, being sorry for sins is a wonderful tool. It is the first step in overcoming the devil and building a better life with God.

Tell the
Good News

How do you get the news in your family? Maybe you get a newspaper, or watch the television, or listen to the radio. There are many ways to find out what is going on in the world. I know of a place where everyone listens to one person who always seems to know what is going on and is glad to tell about it. Sometimes the news is good to hear and sometimes the news is terrible, or just dull.

Jesus had the biggest and best news the world had ever heard. It was what people had been waiting to hear for many, many years. The news was this: God is really ruling the world, the whole earth. It's good news that we can trust God to rule everything because he loves us and will always

---

help us. The good news is called the "Gospel."

Jesus didn't have a newspaper, or radio, or television to use to tell the Gospel. But he knew the best way. He told everyone he met and then asked people like Simon and Andrew and James and John to help him tell people. Soon they were asking still others to help spread the word. Each one told many, and the many told more.

Today Christians are still doing it. The best way to let everyone know about God is to tell the people you meet. Tell the boys and girls you play with: God is our ruler. Tell your friends: God loves you. Jesus asks you to spread the news so everyone soon will know, and believe the Gospel.

Love Is
the Strongest

Some of you boys and girls may know this game. Your parents probably know it and can play with you at home. Then you can play it with your friends. It is a game about which is stronger.

Rock is strong *(make a fist)* so it can break scissors *(stick out fingers to make "scissors")*, but scissors can cut paper *(hold hand out flat)*, and also the paper is stronger than the rock because it can cover a rock. Two or three can play. The way you do it is to put your hands behind your back and each one at the same time brings out his hand as rock, scissors or paper. Since each one is stronger than something else, you can see who wins.

That's a game, but many boys and girls try to show they

Scripture: Mark 1:21-28

Object: *the game "Rock, Scissors, Paper"*

---

are stronger in different ways. Some swing upside down from a tree branch. Some fight. Some yell loudly. Some cry in order to get their way. And some do nasty things. They may get their way for a little while and think they are stronger, but they don't finally win. Jesus shows us what the strongest thing in the world is: the love of God.

That is why Jesus is so strong, he loves the most. The power of Jesus is to love and to serve. Remember, he loved us so much he even died for us.

We follow Jesus. We believe and know that loving and serving others like Jesus did is the strongest thing in the world.

A Way to Say,
"I Love You"

There are many ways to make people feel good, but there is one week of the year I know that many people get to feel better. *(Show the heart.)* They get a big lift in their life because someone cares enough to say, "I love you." People send (Valentine) cards or give others candy or flowers in order to tell them they are loved. Isn't it nice, boys and girls, when someone loves you? It is nicer still when you care enough to love someone else. Love makes you happy, even when other things do not.

It is not just the cards and candy that help. Sometimes a smile gives someone a lift. Sometimes love is shown when there is someone new and you say "Hi" or give them a friendly handshake, or ask them to join in your game. You

Scripture: Mark 1:29-39

Object: *a large red heart (or Valentine candy box)*

---

see, girls and boys, God wants to give everyone praise and joy, and he gives them faith to carry through times when they're sad by showing them that he loves them.

Jesus went around lifting people's spirits by healing and helping, by noticing them and telling them about God. That's why people looked for Jesus wherever he went, because when he talked about God they knew deep down that everything was going to be all right.

That's a good idea! We can say "I love you" not only by candy and sending cards, or by being friendly and kind. We can be like Jesus and tell every person we care about, "God loves you, too." That ought to make them all very glad.

Don't Wait
to Help

Do you remember the last time you were sick? You said, "I don't feel good," and very quickly mommy or daddy paid a lot of attention to you. They got out the thermometer and checked your temperature. Maybe you had to stay in bed all day. Maybe you got to watch TV all day. I'm sure your parents were careful about what you ate, perhaps it was a special soup, or crackers, or something you really like a lot.

I've known girls and boys to get presents when they were sick; coloring books, reading books, games and toys. Sometimes they get cards in the mail that say, "Get Well Quick!"

We know that it's not good to be sick, but we also know that when we are sick we quickly get special attention and extra love.

Scripture: Mark 1:40-45

Object: *fever thermometer (or other equipment used in illness)*

In the reading for today we hear about a sick man who came to Jesus. Jesus didn't wait around once he saw that the man was not well. Right away he said, "I really want you to be well again, and very quickly." I'm sure Jesus isn't any happier when we're sick than we are. He cares about us. Right away he wants to do something about it, just as he did for the man. He wants us to get better.

I suppose this tells us one more thing. If we see other people who are sick, or need help in some way, we shouldn't wait around to see how it turns out. If we can help, we should do something. We can pray for them or quickly show them special love just like Jesus shows to us.

Jesus Tells
the Secret

(Call for a volunteer.) Here, see if you can get them apart. ... Now watch. This is the way to do it. *(Demonstrate. Let at least one child do it successfully.)*

You say there's a trick to it. Well, it's no trick, it's just in knowing how it works and what to do. Once you know the way it works, the whole thing is very easy.

That is true about a lot of things. Maybe you have learned how to drive a nail or bake something good to eat. How hard it seemed at first, until you were told what to do and how it works. Then with some practice it goes quite easily.

The man in the story today was very sick. He couldn't walk, his legs didn't work right. So his friends asked Jesus for help. None of the ways they had tried seemed to work. They were very surprised when the first thing Jesus did was

Scripture: Mark 2:1-12

Object: *a puzzle, such as separating bent nails, etc.*

---

to tell the man his sins were forgiven. He told him that he could be very close to God. Then, when the man knew he was close to God, Jesus told him he could walk again. And he did walk again.

Jesus knew what he was doing because he knows how life works, just as we learned how the puzzle works. It is no secret, no trick. Once you know it, many wonderful things happen. Jesus tells us that what we have done wrong does not keep us from being close to God. God still loves us very much.

We might say Jesus tells us the secret of life. Knowing that God loves and forgives us. That helps us feel right and act right. Now you know the secret, too.

Who Gets
the Attention?

Today, boys and girls, I brought some glue to take care of these cups. Now let's see we have to put the glue in the right places and then they'll be okay again.

(Pick up the good cup) Hmm, I wonder where I should put the glue on this cup.... Here? ... Or here? Oh, you probably think I'm silly trying to put glue on a perfectly good cup. You don't have to fix a cup that's not broken. It is beautiful the way it is; useful and a pleasure for everyone. Let's set that here to enjoy it.

(Pick up the broken cup) Ah, *this* is the one that needs the attention. *(Mend cup with some fussing.)* Yes, this takes time to do it right.... I wonder, if I were that good cup over there what I'd be thinking? Do you think I'd say, "Look at that other fellow. He gets all the attention and I sit here and no one even bothers with me?" I don't think so. I think that cup would say, "Boy, am I glad I'm not broken. I'm still in one piece. I can be polished better and be more useful." Yes sir, rather than getting attention I'd rather never be broken at all.

Scripture: Mark 2:13-17

Object: *two cups, one of which is broken, and mending cement*

Maybe there have been times when you've been good and it seemed that the bad boys and girls get all the attention. Or when you're feeling fine and you notice that boys and girls who feel sad or hurt seem to have teachers and parents always doing things for them. I've even known boys and girls to be bad or pretend to be sick just to get people to notice them.

In today's lesson, Jesus is eating with the very worst people in town and the good people hardly get to see him. Jesus tells these good people, "It's the broken cup that needs the fixing, so I'm giving lots of extra loving to these sinners." I'd rather never be broken and always be beautiful and useful for God and for others.

This tells us something else. If we are ever hurt or sad, or when we do need help in getting fixed up because we've done something wrong, or if there is something we just can't seem to do right, God will give us all the extra love and help we need to get better and be beautiful again.

A Time
to Be Happy

What could be more fun than birthdays? I'm sure you remember your last birthday and almost every boy and girl knows about how long it will be until another birthday comes along.

Birthdays are happy times. You have balloons and presents, a big cake with candles on it, maybe your favorite food. Some girls and boys get to go to their favorite place on their birthdays. But very often you have a party. That is because you want everyone to be happy and share all the happiness you feel.

There are things you do on birthdays and there are things you don't do. You aren't ever sad. There is hardly any way to be sad at a time like that. It just doesn't fit. Sad things just get set aside until that time is over.

Today I want to tell you about another happy time. It

Scripture: Mark 2:18-22

Object: *birthday party hat, or decorations, or a cake with candles*

---

was the time when Jesus was with his disciples. Some people said to Jesus, "You never tell your disciples to be sad about the world. Why aren't they being gloomy when everyone else is?" "Oh," said Jesus, "there are times to be sad, but when I am with the disciples they can't be sad."

And that's true! When Jesus is with us we know how much God loves us and how we belong to him. How can anybody be sad then? People who worry about whether God loves them might be sad, and people who think they have to work hard in order for God to love them might be sad, but people who know Jesus don't have to worry or prove anything to God. They know God really cares for them.

Boys and girls, Jesus is with us now. Why, this surely is a time to be happy!

Rules
or People?

I suppose many of you have seen your parents use a map like this when you travel. If you're going on vacation or going to visit someone having a road map is a big help. It is like a picture of the road you travel on. It tells you when the road will turn and in what direction. It tells you the name of towns and parks, of lakes and mountains. It tells you how far it is between places. It is like a law, it tells you exactly how things are.

It is important to have a map if you're going on a vacation, but the map doesn't make the vacation. Most important is the people. If people are happy and fun to be with, if they like to travel and enjoy seeing things, *that's* what makes a good trip. Don't you love it when Daddy takes a different road to go see something you want to see, or stops to get

Scripture: Mark 2:23-28

Object: *a road map*

---

ice cream, even if that wasn't planned? The best maps in the world aren't as important as people.

Jesus always respects the law. He knew the rules are good for us but he knew the rules aren't as important as the people who use them. Maybe you have a time to go to bed, but sometimes if you're tired you may go to bed earlier. You may know how much money you should give to church on Sunday, but sometimes to thank God you may give more than that. You know it's not polite to interrupt people who are speaking, but if something important happens like if someone gets hurt you may have to start talking right away.

That's why we listen to the Lord Jesus and try to be like him. He loves people so much that he knows exactly what to do, even when the law doesn't tell us. Rules are fine, but being a good person and loving others is really what counts.

What Makes You Mad?

I have a toy here I thought you would enjoy seeing. *(Describe what it does.)* This one is especially funny. *(Turn it on.)* . . . Oh, let me try it again. . . . I thought I'd checked it out. . . . It doesn't seem to work. Now doesn't that make you mad!

Maybe that's happened to you, too. You think about what fun something would be and then it doesn't work. Or you go out to ride your bike and a tire is flat. Or you switch on the television and the picture won't come on. Most of us get angry when we're disappointed like that, usually because we can't have something we wanted. Of course, that's pretty selfish. A wise man once said you can tell about a person if you know what it is that makes him angry.

Scripture: Mark 3:1-6

Object: *a toy that does not work (with worn-out batteries)*

Did you know that Jesus got angry, too? Jesus got angry when he saw what illness had done to one of God's children. He knew God wants everyone to be well and able to work. But what made him really angry was when he saw that some people didn't care. They were more interested in telling Jesus what he did wrong than in helping someone. Jesus just went ahead and helped the sick man more. He healed him.

You see, boys and girls, God made us to have good bodies and minds. God always wants us to be healthy. He doesn't like to see us not well. But what makes him angry is when people don't care that others need help. That ought to make us angry, too. Angry enough to help.

Jesus Is
for Everyone

I think everyone knows what this is. Who can tell us? (*Allow a child to respond.*) Yes, it's a bottle of Coke. It's something almost everyone has tasted and all but a very few really like it.

You know that's true in your family. Maybe you know all your friends like it, too. But did you know you can get it all over the whole world? Girls and boys in far-away countries like this drink, know its name, and use it to be refreshed. It's sold in Europe and Africa, in South America and Japan, just about everywhere. It seems to be one thing we all agree on.

It seemed that just about everyone agreed about Jesus when he was teaching and preaching also. People from many different countries were glad to see him, and wherever he went there were crowds of people around.

Scripture: Mark 3:7-19a

Object: *a bottle of Coca-Cola*

When Jesus chose his closest disciples he chose all kinds of people. Some were fishermen, another worked with money, some wanted to change the government and some didn't, some were rich, some were poor, some spoke loudly and others were quiet. But they all agreed that Jesus cared about them and they were happy when he called them to work with him.

You see, boys and girls, even more than this drink is for everyone, Jesus is truly for everyone. He cares about you whether you are sick or well, whether you are bad or good, whether you feel beautiful or feel ugly. It doesn't make any difference how you feel about yourself or even what other people think. Jesus loves you. That's why it feels good to be close to Jesus. He is for everyone. He is for you.

Choosing Sides

Remember the last time you and your friends were getting ready to play a game? One of the first things you did was choose up sides. Two of you were made captains to pick the players. And they'd start. I want John . . . I'll take Mike . . . Let's see . . . Lisa . . . Bill . . . Walt . . . Mary. . . .

What were they thinking of? Who was the strongest. Who could throw far. And you saw the teams shaping up. If you were not called yet you knew which team was better. Maybe when the captain you wanted to be with was picking, you jumped up and down and waved and said, "Pick me, pick me." Yes sir, you knew which team you'd rather be on. You knew the people you wanted to play with. And when you were picked you probably joined in telling your captain who else should be picked with you.

In some ways, being a Christian is like choosing which side you are on. Christians are people who know how strong

Scripture: Mark 3:20-35

Object: *playground ball or ball and bat*

---

and good God is and so they want to be on God's side. They know Jesus is on God's side and he is as strong as one can be. He knows what God wants done and everyone on his team knows what God wants done, and they do it.

Jesus fights evil and wrong; all Christians fight evil. Jesus helps the sick; Christians help the sick. Jesus is a friend to lonely people; Christians are friends to lonely people. Jesus doesn't hold grudges; Christians don't hold grudges. Jesus is kind; Christians are kind.

I can't imagine why anybody would want to be on a side against God! I can't imagine why anybody would want to be on God's team and then *not* want to do what he wants! It is when you do what God wants done, when you do what Jesus does, that you are on God's side. What could be better than that?

Listening

Do you know there is music being played and words being spoken all around us right now? Of course, you can't hear it, but I have brought something to help us listen. *(Show radio.)* It's a radio. The radio is something that will help us hear the signals that are all around us. We weren't listening a few minutes ago, now we can listen. If we turn it on *(turn it on)* . . . ah, we hear the music.

Isn't it nice to listen to the radio? It tells you about things going on, plays music, has important news, and is even a kind of friend if you're alone. Those things are always there, but of course, we must be listening. If we've turned it off we can't hear the message.

Maybe you remember times when you wanted to listen to the radio and things got in the way. Maybe there was a storm and the sound was filled with static so you had to listen extra hard. Or maybe you had your radio on but there were other noises in the room and you could hardly hear what it was saying. Or you were listening and someone said

Scripture: Mark 4:1-20

Object: *transistor radio*

---

something to you and you answered, and missed the song. I remember times when I wanted to hear the weather report and kept the radio on to hear it, but I realized too late that it had been given and I just wasn't paying attention.

This is what Jesus tells us about God's message to us—his Word. It is always there. God is showing us all the time that he loves us and saves us. God always wants us to know Jesus and to tell other boys and girls about our Lord. But so often we're not turned on to listen.

Even when we are in a place where we can listen and intend to listen other things get in the way. In church or Sunday school we start thinking about other things. Or we go out saying, "I'm going to remember God this week," and soon we are busy playing and doing things, and God never gets thought of.

God's Word is wonderful and good for us. God always has a good message for us. But we must listen, even if other things get in the way. A Christian always listens to God.

The Word:
One at a Time

Do you remember the first time you saw a box of tissues like this? You took a tissue and *(pull one)* another popped up. Wow, you pulled again and another came up. What fun! Of course that is wasteful if you don't need the tissues. I'm going to fold these and use them. I remember hearing of a mother who came into a room which had tissues all over it because a very little boy had found that they popped out and had pulled out every one of them.

Finding out about God in his Word is something like using these tissues. There is a little of it showing, and when you see that using the Word is indeed helpful, you begin to take it and use it. *(Take tissue out slowly.)* Of course what is important is not only that you take—listen to—the Word of God but that you *use* it. So when we hear God's Word, let's say when he tells us to be friendly, we use that Word, be friendly, and find out how good that is.

Scripture: Mark 4:21-25

Object: *box of tissues with pop-up folding feature*

After you have once used the Word, you discover that it can be used not only for one thing, but for many things. So you go back and sure enough the Word is waiting. Maybe this time you are sick and the Word tells you that God cares for you. *(Pull tissue.)* And that is good, too. Then you hear that God wants us to be generous and share things. *(Pull tissue.)* Then it's a Word that teaches us to use our world well and not be careless and wasteful. *(Pull tissue.)*

It seems that the more you use the Word of God the more there is to use. Because God wants to show and tell us many things, there is always more. So we receive the Word one thing at a time, and when we use and practice doing what he says, then we can go back to him for the next one.

Remember, if we don't use it, we'll not get any more.

That's the way the Word works: listen, use it, and go back for more, for as long as you live. One at a time.

Great Nation,
Greater Kingdom

Look at all the stars on this flag! Does anyone know how many there are? ... Yes, fifty stars. Each star stands for a different state of the United States of America. That is a lot of states, especially when you remember that when the United States started there were only thirteen.

That reminds us how much bigger the United States is today than when it started. People are very proud that this nation which once seemed so little is now one of the biggest nations in the whole world. One of the ways it became big and strong was that it took many different kinds of people who all became citizens. People from North Europe and South Europe, people from Arabian lands and Jews, people from India and China, people from Africa and from the West Indies, all kinds of people were welcome to be part of the nation—and that made it great.

Boys and girls, we belong to a nation which is even greater than this United States. We belong to the kingdom of God

Scripture: Mark 4:26-34

Object: *USA national flag*

---

which includes all the people who trust God through Jesus. Jesus reminds us that the kingdom of God also seemed small once, too. When Jesus was on earth it seemed that there were just a few people who believed him. Jesus knew that many, many more people were to be saved by believing. God would make the kingdom grow.

He told his few disciples to go out and find others to tell them about Jesus. And sure enough, the kingdom grew and grew. Today there are people from all over the world in God's kingdom. People with dark skins and light skins, people in Asia and in America, people in every country and of every type. And God's kingdom is still growing because Christians keep on telling others about Jesus. We do the telling, God makes it grow.

It is really wonderful to be in a great nation. It is wonderful to be in the *greater* kingdom of God.

Strength
We Trust

Today I asked Jerry to bring some weights he uses for exercise. *(Make a show of moving heavy weights or bar into view.)* I wonder whether several of you would like to come up here to help lift these? *(Have children or group attempt to move weights.)* These sure are heavy. Jerry will you come and show us how you lift these? *(Respond to lifting with appropriate remark over being impressed.)*

Now that is being strong, isn't it? I'll bet any one of you girls or boys would be glad to allow Jerry to lift you up or to hold something for you. If he said he'd lift me to reach something, I'd surely trust him because he's so strong. Whenever we see someone strong, right away we trust that person.

I'm sure that is the way the disciples felt when they saw Jesus handle that terrible storm on the sea. Of course they could see he was like God standing up and telling the storm to be quiet. I mean, have you ever felt a wind blow strong

Scripture: Mark 4:35-41

Object: *young athlete with weights (bar bells)*

---

with rain and have you ever seen it bend the trees? Sometimes it pushes you right down from the street. What strength, to make the storm be still! They saw that was like God. Right away they trusted him.

Boys and girls, we see a lot of big and strong things in the world; the bright, bright sun which God sends every day; the weight of winter snow; the strength of swift water in a river; someone getting over being sick and getting strength again. These and many more things show how strong God is, and that he uses his strength to save and protect us. Even when Jesus died and rose again we can see the strength of God.

It surely seems to me that if we trust strong young men, then more than that we can trust Jesus. Yes, we *do* trust Jesus.

Something
to Tell

Once in a while you get something that is really nice. A toy, a new bike, or some shoes, or something like this. At first you keep it for yourself to play with or look at, but one day a friend is playing at your house and sees it, or you bring it outside. "Oh," everyone says, "that's really nice." It makes you feel good to have something other people admire.

Then someone says, "Where did you get it?" Now what do you say? Do you say, "It's a secret and I'm not telling," or "I'd rather not talk about that," or "Don't you wish you knew"? No, right away you tell them who gave it to you or the store where you bought it, because that way they can get one, too.

In our story for today we hear about a man who was very sick, and everyone knew how sick he was. People used to talk about that man and even stay away from him. But Jesus came and cured him. At one time he wouldn't talk to any-

Scripture: Mark 5:1-20

Object: *any popularly advertised toy or gay stuffed animal*

---

one and would howl all the time, but now he could talk. And what a story he had to talk about! It was how God had made him well because Jesus cared about him and came to him.

At first he said to Jesus, "Let me go away with you," but Jesus had a better idea. He said, "Why don't you go back to those people who knew how sick you were and tell them about God's mercy? They need to know that." So right away the man did just that. Soon everyone knew about God's love because of what he told.

Girls and boys, when you have something wonderful, you want people to know about it. And God has been good to you too. You know he loves you. You know Jesus. You go to a Sunday school and church. That's even better than toys. That's something everyone ought to know. Don't keep it to yourself. Tell your friends how good God is.

A Glimpse
of Glory

Do you remember the last time you had a party? Maybe it was your birthday party, and just when you were ready to blow out the candles someone said, "Hold it!" lifted a camera and took a picture. *(Take a picture, just the click or a flash going off is enough.)* Then you knew you had a picture of that great moment.

Suppose you were a little person inside the camera. You couldn't see anything outside in the big world. Then, just for that click a place opened up and you could see the happy party, people, balloons, and candles, and then it closed up again. Somehow you would be happier in that camera knowing that there was so much more to life. And what is more, you'd have a picture to keep and remind you always of that joy.

In a way, boys and girls, this beautiful story of the little girl who was sick, died, and who Jesus returned to life, is a quick glimpse of God's great life. You see, everybody said, "Oh she is dead, there is nothing more to be done."

Scripture: Mark 5:21-24a, 35-43

Object: *a camera*

Everybody, that is, except the girl's father. He asked Jesus and Jesus saw more than anyone. He knew there is much more to God's life than we see. So he said to the father, "Trust me."

Sure enough, where everyone saw death, Jesus saw life, and just for that one time he showed that life to everyone. He spoke to the girl and she got up. That is a quick little picture of one very happy moment when we can see the life God has for all of us.

Maybe there have been other times when everyone was sad and felt that nothing could be good again. Maybe it was when someone died or when no one understood how you felt or when things were terribly wrong. But boys and girls, Jesus can see more than we. Here we have a snapshot of what he sees. Just what he said to that father, he says to us, "Trust me." This one time we got to see what Jesus sees always—a great life from God. It is like having a picture of a great good time. Why, we don't ever have to be sad again!

What Happens Inside?

I wonder how many boys and girls have watched their mother make a cake? Maybe some of you have helped her or even done most of it yourself. Do you remember what you do?

First you take the flour and other mixings in a bowl, then put in liquid such as milk and eggs, and you mix them. Soon you have a runny stuff we call batter. It's sort of thick and gooey and really not very good to eat. Then you put it in a pan and into the oven. A marvelous thing happens. That thick and gooey stuff dries out and when it comes out it is light and fluffy, and oh so good.

What happened? Well, you say, we baked it. Yes, the heat was on the outside. Have you ever broken a piece of cake open and looked very closely? There are tiny air holes all through it. We needed the heat of the oven but what happened *inside* the cake was important. You can't watch it happen, but if you want to know what made it good you have to know what happened inside.

Scripture: Mark 5:24b-34

Object: *a cake*

When the woman in the story came to Jesus she was not well. She was unhappy with herself. She knew she needed Jesus, like the batter needs the oven. So she came to him and got just as close to him as she could. Sure enough, when she got near to Jesus she got well through and through. Jesus then said a surprising thing: he said to her, "It wasn't just that you got near and touched me. Look inside yourself. You believed me and you believe God. It was what happened inside you that made the difference."

Girls and boys, coming to church and Sunday school is very important. Often we are near Jesus when we think about him during the days of the week, when we say our prayers, when we hear stories from the Bible, when we just remember him. That is truly fine. That is the outside. But what happens inside is that we believe Jesus and trust him. Then we become happy with ourselves because he loves us. That is what makes the difference. When we believe Jesus we are better inside . . . all the way through.

Don't
Overlook God

Look at the things there are in this small bit of earth! What do you see? ... There are so many things. Leaves, bugs, flowers, etc. All these things right here. And just think, boys and girls, when we walk along outside there is so much of this that we hardly think of what beautiful things are living right next to us. It is just so ordinary we don't think of the life God has placed right there in a little piece of ground.

It is not only in such little things that life gets overlooked. Have you ever felt that nobody noticed you? Maybe you have an older brother or sister and it seems that when he or she speaks everyone listens, but nobody listens to you. Maybe you had something exciting happen once and you ran in to tell about it but everybody was busy with other things and didn't hear you. Maybe you are an older brother or sister and it seems like you've been around so long everyone pays attention to the little ones.

Sometimes when a new boy or girl comes to live in your neighborhood nobody plays with him or her. It's really too

Scripture: Mark 6:1-6

Object: *a piece of ground with mosses, tiny flowers, bugs, etc., which children can gather around to see.*

---

bad to miss knowing a good friend. Someone has to notice and go over and get acquainted. Yes, so often we miss life when it is right up close to us.

Did you realize that the same thing happened to Jesus? He was bringing God's own message to people. In fact, God himself was healing people through Jesus. What did people say? "Oh, that's just Jesus. We know his brothers and sisters and mother. We don't believe him."

Wasn't that a shame? They forgot that God's gifts come right close in ordinary life; that every day it is in the people around us that God is showing his life—in tiny creatures, in our family, school and at play.

Yes, boys and girls, we know how sad it is to overlook someone. There isn't much we can do about other people when they don't see others or God, but we can do something. We can keep our eyes open to God's wonderful gifts—we can be friendly, we can listen to others, we can see God.

You Can
Do It Yourself

Do you remember how hard it used to be to get dressed? Now sometimes you still need help, but it seemed so difficult when you were really little. You couldn't get shoes on right, socks never seemed to be straight. And shirts. Shirts with buttons are the hardest of all. First you have to find which side is out and which sleeve is on which side. Then the buttons have to fit into the right holes. Do you remember how good you felt when you didn't have to wait for mommy to button your clothes? Do you remember how great it was when after many tries you could say, "I can do it myself"?

So often we have to listen and learn for a long time before we're allowed to do things ourselves. Maybe it's crossing the street, or turning channels on the television, pouring the milk, or someday driving a car. For all these we watch someone who does it well, and we learn, and then try it ourselves.

This story today from Mark tells of one of those great days when people do something themselves for the first time. The twelve apostles had been listening to Jesus for many months. They saw him heal the sick and help people. Most of all

Scripture: Mark 6:7-13

Object: *a child's shirt with buttons*

---

they saw him tell everyone that they should be ready to let God rule their lives. "Repent," Jesus had told people, "and believe the good news of God's love for you."

This was the big day. Jesus said to his disciples, "You can do it yourself." Some wondered whether they were ready, but soon they all went out to tell people about God's care and a new way to live for God. They just talked and helped others as Jesus had done. It was a great day! But the story doesn't stop there, because after they tried it they found that anyone who knows Jesus can do it. Men and women, boys and girls first listen to Jesus and do as he does. Does it seem hard to tell someone God loves them? No, you can do it yourself. Does it seem hard to smile and be friendly? No, you can do it yourself. Does it seem hard to pray for someone to be better when they are sick? No, you can do it yourself.

Yes, girls and boys, you don't have to wait to be big or old to do many things that are really important for Christians—telling and helping. Because you listen to Jesus, you know now you can do it yourself.

Jesus Shows
His Love

Have you ever come into the house after playing and said, "Mom, what's for supper?" You expect that she will answer and tell you the kind of food she has prepared, the meat and vegetables and so forth. You don't come in and say, "Mom, are you going to let us eat tonight?" You know that somehow your parents will see that there is something to eat. Maybe you haven't thought about that because, of course, your parents take care of you. It is part of loving you. When you say, "What's for supper," it is really like saying, "I know you love me and will take care of me. I trust you to care enough."

Parents do more than feed you because they love you. They take care of you in many ways. They get you clothes. They protect you. They would even do without something themselves, if they had to, to get you something you really needed. The food for supper is just a sign of all those things.

When Jesus was way out in the country, far from any towns, with people who were hungry, we are told that he made sure they had something to eat. That's really great that Jesus would even care about getting supper for those people. It shows how powerful he is, but it shows a lot more. If he would feed them, he loves them enough to take care of them in other ways, too. He cares enough to teach them about God. He cares enough to teach how to live better. Indeed, Jesus even is willing to die for them because they need that. He gives himself to everyone.

You remember how before we eat we say thank you to God for giving us the food. Really we could say, "Thank you for the food, thank you for loving us, thank you for everything, and most of all, thank you for Jesus."

I Don't
Understand

Everyone here has listened to a watch. You put it up to your ear and listen ... tick, tick, tick. That's really something, a little piece of jewelry like this which makes a sound which is so nice to listen to. Of course, a watch does more than tick, it also tells us the time. When we want to know what the time is we can look at the hands and see where they are pointing. That tells us what time it is.

So a watch is useful and helpful, and a watch is fun to listen to. But do you know how it works? It is best not to take one apart by yourself but maybe someone in your family will take the back off one for you to see. Inside are lots and lots of tiny wheels with bumps on them we call cogs, and each one is a gear. These wheels go around and fit together in ways I don't understand. I am amazed that they keep going so well, but they do. All day long and all night they keep going around, tick, tick, tick, and I can tell the time.

Scripture: Mark 6:45-52

Object: *a watch*

You see, boys and girls, I do not have to understand all about how watches work to tell the time, all I have to do is read it.

There are things I don't understand about God, also. I know that God takes care of us. I know that when we get sick we get well again. I know that even when things seem scary, God is watching to make sure we're all right. I don't understand how he takes care of every person all the time. All day long and all night God keeps us all safe in his love. He makes everything fit together for our good, like the gears in the watch.

It is like the watch we can use without understanding it. We can trust God even when we don't know how he does it. It is enough to know that we are always safe in his loving care.

One Touch
Is Enough

Some things you always remember. I brought this today because every girl and every boy remembers what it is like to have a big scoop of ice cream and to lick it. It softly melts all over your tongue and its sweet goodness comes in and makes you feel good as its taste seems to go into your whole self. You're not satisfied with one lick, but once you've had a lick you know exactly what it is like. I bet even now you can just think of what it feels like to lick an ice cream cone.

There are other things like that. Have you ever held a puppy and had its happy squiggly fuzzy warmth wiggle in your arms? If you have, you know just from that one time how good it feels. Maybe you have gotten to jump into a big pile of straw or of leaves and had it almost cover you up. Whee, it's great! You may get to do it again, but once is enough to know what it feels like. Remembering it makes you feel all good again.

You know, this happened when people met Jesus. Jesus,

Scripture: Mark 6:53-56

Object: *cone for ice cream (or candle shaped like an ice cream cone)*

---

when he walked around, was so great and so good that people gathered all around him, and as he talked they would sometimes just touch him. It was a touch they would always remember. It was like feeling how strong and how gentle he was. It was a touch so filled with love they would feel it all over. They could never forget its goodness.

We can't reach out and touch Jesus with our hands today, but sometimes we can feel how close Jesus is to us. Maybe it happens at a time when the room is quiet and you are talking to God. Maybe it is when your dad or mom has an arm around you and you think about God. It could be when you make something very nice, or when you see something beautiful. Or it could be when you realize you are very sure that God loves you always. It's something you'll always remember. It may happen again, but knowing Jesus is close to you is so very, very good that once is enough to remember it always.

What Is
Inside?

I brought an apple today. Isn't this a good looking one?
That skin is red and shiny. It is smooth. Oh, see the stem
here. That's firmly attached. And look at the shape, the way
it is round up here and goes in toward the bottom. Yes sir,
that is a fine apple. *(Make as if to set it aside.)*

Oh, I know what you're thinking. You're thinking, "Hey,
you don't know an apple by looking at its skin. That may
be fine but under the skin is the good part." Of course, the
skin is only the outside. If we cut a piece off, *(do it)* then we
see the white part inside. That's the part boys and girls are
interested in. That's the part we eat. It could have a nice
skin and not be firm or sweet to eat. The outside isn't the
important part at all.

And if we asked the apple what is important we would
be told to go deeper. *(Cut it in half.)* There at the heart are

Scripture: Mark 7:1-8, 14-15, 21-23

Object: *an apple and a knife to cut it*

---

the seeds. The outside may be red and the flesh may be good, but the seeds are the real purpose for which the tree made the apple. The question is, "What is deep inside?"

This is what Jesus tells us about our life, too. A lot of people seem to think that what something looks like is all that matters. So they smile and say nice things, but inside they may have hateful thoughts. Maybe they play and look happy, but really they are jealous when they look at other boys and girls. That is really sad.

Jesus wants us to be smiling and to do the right things. He wants us to act friendly and happy. But more than that he wants to be sure our inside, where the seed is, is good. Jesus is the person we look to, to change what is inside us, so we can be good—starting right at the center. Then everything else will be good as well.

Believe in
God's Goodness

Have you ever tried to open one of these? You know, here you are with what looks like it's going to be good. So first you pull it this way, then the other way. Maybe you try to open it with your teeth. Maybe you try to pull the sides apart. *(Be tugging at it all along.)* That's a hard one all right. But I bet if you get one of these you keep at it until that bag is open.

Why do you keep at something, even when it is hard? Because you know that even though it is hard to get at, there is something very good for you at the end. You and I keep at it even though something is very stubborn because we know what is inside is very fine.

Have you ever felt that way about things you ask God for? Maybe it is something you would really like to have. Or I have known boys and girls to ask God to help someone who really needs help. We may pray for a person who is mean, to be smiling and kind. There are times when we wish we weren't afraid of something. If you have done this kind of

Scripture: Mark 7:24-30

Object: *a bag (or box) of candy that is hard for a child to open*

---

thing you know that sometimes even though we pray, it doesn't seem that what we ask for happens. At times like that, we Christians still keep praying and living close to God. Why? Because we know that when God answers it will be very, very nice.

The woman who spoke to Jesus about getting her little girl healed had a hard time. It seemed that everyone got in her way. The disciples told her to go away; even Jesus seemed like a foreign person. But she knew that God's answers are very, very good. She expected her girl to be healed, so she kept at it, asking for help, and the child did become well again.

That's why we keep going as Christians. We keep praying, and helping, and doing things for others even though it is hard. We know that God's love will be with us. It is a struggle *(open bag)* but we believe God will surely bring us good things. Not just candy, but all the things he knows we need.

Things You
Have to Tell

Have you ever tried to keep a secret? The more wonderful it is and the more you think about it, the harder it is to keep.

Let's say it's your mother's birthday, and you and daddy go to the store for a present. You get a bottle of perfume. Daddy says, "Now remember, it's a secret." "Okay," you think, "I'm not going to tell."

Pretty soon you get home and without thinking you say, "I know about your birthday...oops...no I don't." Well, you get by that time. Then you see a friend outside and you say, "We're giving mommy perfume for her birthday. Oh, I'm not supposed to tell anyone." Later you go back into the house and you say, "Gee it smells nice in here...." Agh, you did it again. Maybe later you stop by when your mother is combing her hair and you say, "You don't have many bottles on your dresser, do you?"

You know, when you know a wonderful thing it just won't

Scripture: Mark 7:31-37

Object: *a bottle for perfume*

---

stay inside. It keeps popping out because it is so exciting and good.

When Jesus had performed a miracle the people around him couldn't help but keep talking about it. He even told them not to say anything, but it was so exciting they told everyone.

That's the wonderful thing we have, too. We have the Holy Spirit, the love of Jesus in our lives. We know the news that Jesus died and rose for us, that we can trust him always to take care of us. All that is inside and when you know it, it keeps popping out.

Sometimes you tell a friend about Jesus. Sometimes it comes out when you're feeling happy. Sometimes you just think it, "Jesus loves me." That's the surprise and delight of being a Christian.

Enough—
and Leftovers

You will all recognize what this is for. You know when you have a meal at home and some of the meat or vegetables is left over, your mother puts it in one of these to keep it for another meal.

Jesus didn't have plastic containers for the leftovers that day he fed the crowd by the sea, but when they were finished the disciples carefully gathered the leftovers so God's gift of food would not be wasted. But isn't it marvelous, girls and boys, that we *have* leftovers? I mean that we have so much that even after we're full, there is more.

I'm not thinking only of food. Sometimes we think we'd like more of this or that, but truly, God has given us more than we can use. All the sunshine there is which we will

Scripture: Mark 8:1-10

Object: *a plastic refrigerator leftover container*

---

never see; the great amount of land we have, land we can't use; there is more grass than we can look at; and streams that splash and babble without anyone to hear them. There are more chairs at home to sit on than there are people to sit. There are more clothes than you can wear.

Think of all the love in the world! There are so many people who would want you as their friend. Why, I imagine everyone here can think of several things you have more than enough of.

That's the way God is. When he gives us things he sees that there is enough, and leftovers. How good God is! How much he must love us!

Signs
of God

Some of you boys and girls already know how to read the traffic signs your Dad and Mother watch when they drive the car. Do you know what this one says? . . . It says, "Stop." It is made in a special shape, it is red and it has big letters so no one will miss it. What are some other signs on the roads? *(Elicit various traffic signs.)* Yes, and whenever they are put up they are big so no one will miss them.

I wonder if you realize that God also puts signs up in the world? Not signs which tell us what to do, but signs that tell us God is all around. Of course, God's signs aren't in big letters, but they are there for everyone to see. The only reason some people miss them is they are looking for the wrong things. God does not shout at us, "Hey, look at me,"

Scripture: Mark 8:11-13

Object: Stop *sign or other traffic sign*

---

and he doesn't always make us amazed. Instead his signs are put all over in quiet and beautiful ways.

When you see a bird fly, getting food and water, chirping away, that's a sign of God. When you see a pretty flower to enjoy, that's a sign of God. When you eat lunch and it tastes good, that's a sign of God. When you feel you can love or be loved, that's a sign, too. When you have a friend to hold hands with, or to talk to, that's a sign. When someone gets over being sick, that is God again.

You see, girls and boys, God has left signs all over for you and me to see how God is around. When you know God and his love you know what to look for. Then, it seems, the whole world is just full of God.

Understanding
Life

What would you think if you saw this for the first time? Let's see, what is it for? Is it a dish? Is it a hat? Maybe a small sled. That's a puzzle. Everyone who has one seems glad to have it, but what does it do?

I might decide it is a dish. Then, of course, I would always have trouble with it. Oh, that dish of mine doesn't stand straight. It keeps tipping over. It doesn't hold very much. I might even worry about my dish. I certainly wouldn't enjoy having it.

You all know this is a Frisbee. It is meant to be enjoyed and used. Once you have learned how to use it, you'd do it very differently. I had it upside down. It is made to throw.

Scripture: Mark 8:14-21

Object: *a frisbee*

When you know what it is for, and how it works, it is really great.

How much Jesus wants us to understand about life! All around there are people who are using it all wrong. When you do, life is puzzling and hard. If you try to be bossy, people don't help you. If you are grumpy and shout, everyone seems grumpy. If you are always afraid, everything looks scary. If you think life is for getting rather than giving, it won't work well.

But we know how life works. We know we can trust God. We don't have to be afraid. We can smile and be happy. We have learned to love our neighbor and help others. We understand. Life is to be used and enjoyed, with God.

Giving
Quietly

Today I want you boys and girls to count something. I'm going to look at my watch and I'd like for you to count how many times you took in a breath, just sitting there and breathing as you always do. I'll tell you when to start counting the breaths you take in, and when to stop. Okay? Start counting now . . . *(wait fifteen seconds)* . . . stop.

How many did you take in? How many people took in eight breaths? Raise your hands. More than eight? Seven breaths? six? Five? Fewer than five? Wow! Do you realize that every fifteen seconds all of you boys and girls take in *(do some quick arithmetic)* ____breaths? Think of all the breaths we take in, in a day. Why even while we're sleeping we breathe and all that good air comes in.

That air is a gift from God. That's something God has put

Scripture: Mark 8:22-26

Object: *counting the number of breaths we take in 15 seconds*

---

here for everyone, and we all use it, over and over again. Nobody says "Thank you" but God keeps giving it to us. He gives it so quietly and so often that we don't mention it very much, but it is always there.

That is just like Jesus. Sometimes it was someone who needed healing. Sometimes it was someone who needed to hear a kind word. Sometimes it was someone who had to be told how to do something. Jesus loved to do it quietly; he just wanted the person helped.

Don't you think that's a good way to give? How beautiful it is to give quietly, just for the joy that someone is helped. It would seem Jesus would want us to do the same thing. To help and to give like God, quietly.

Jesus Is
the Christ

One of the ways you can tell what people do is by looking at the hats they are wearing. If you saw someone with this hat, you'd say, "You are a fireman." With this hat you would know a construction worker. Or with this . . . a nurse. *(The children can be asked to identify them.)* Sure, if someone wears a hat you can tell right away what that person does.

Sometimes it's the other way around. It isn't until you see what they are doing that you know what their job is. A truck driver doesn't look different until he drives a truck. You know someone is a teacher when they go to school and teach a class. Even the president of the United States looks the same as any businessman. It is what they *do* that makes them special.

Jesus didn't wear anything special to show he was chosen

Scripture: Mark 8:27-35

Object: *two or three hats from various occupations*

---

to do God's work; so just looking at Jesus he seemed like any other man of his day. He walked and dressed like everyone else. He ate food and went to bed like everyone else. It was when Jesus started doing things that people could tell he was different. He helped people more than anyone. He was stronger, yet more gentle, than anyone. Most of all, what he taught about God was so true, so right, that soon everyone knew he was God's own messenger.

Jesus was, and is, more than that. St. Peter said he was God's special messenger who had come to be our savior. It is what he does that tells us who he is. He came to die for us and to rise again. Yes, Jesus is someone very special indeed.

Directions
for Use

Did you ever have a game like this? Perhaps you remember when you first opened it up. There was the board, and the pieces, the cards, the dice. Oh, here's a little thing, what is that for? After you looked at all the pieces I bet you asked a question, "How do you play?" Because, of course, having all the pieces doesn't mean much if you don't know what to do with them.

How do you find out how to play? *(Wait for response.)* Sure, you look at the rules. There it says who goes first, how the pieces are used, what wins and how you get there. It tells you what to do and what not to do if the game is going to be fun for everyone. It certainly helps to have directions.

Jesus has given us some helpful direction, not for a game,

Scripture: Mark 8:34-38

Object: *boxed game, with directions (or rule book for a sport)*

---

but for life. He makes life, so he knows how to use it best. He says you have to be willing to lose your life if you are really going to enjoy it. He says that getting things may really get in the way of enjoying life. I know it doesn't seem as if that would be so, it seems to some people that getting more things for yourself would make you happier. But Jesus knows the best directions, and he says, "Forget yourself and serve others."

The most important direction for life is to be proud of knowing Jesus. That is really the biggest thing. If you know and love Jesus, and try to live like he lives, life will turn out to be great. Follow his directions. He knows.

Something to Help Us Remember

I'm sure you remember the times you were at the fair or at a carnival or at the circus. You remember the rides you went on—round and round—and what fun it was. Remember you could wave to your family and they waved back. You had things to eat, popcorn, hot dogs. You saw things. Maybe you saw animals doing tricks or beautiful cattle. Maybe you saw acrobats doing stunts or an aerialist way high up. What things there are to remember!

Of course most of that is all over. The rides are over, the tricks have been done, the animals are gone and the popcorn is all eaten *(show empty box)*. But maybe you won a prize *(show doll, or toy)* or a medal or a pennant to help you remember. It brings back all the good times and helps you look forward to the next time. Until then, it's one way to remember and keep some of the happiness.

The disciples with Jesus also saw a wonderful and marvelous thing which was as great for them as any fair has

Scripture: Mark 9:2-9

Object: *kewpie doll (or stuffed toy), empty popcorn box*

---

been to us. It was when, for a few minutes, they saw the real glory of God shine in Jesus. I mean, he glowed, God spoke, and Moses and Elijah were there. It was one of those great times you always want to remember.

But they, and we, need something to help us keep remembering. Peter tried to think of something and suggested they build little houses on the mountain, because that certainly is not a place to have a pennant. God also knew he would have to give us something to remember such a good thing with, so he gave us something which is always with us. He leaves us his Word. All the things which Jesus does and says, and Jesus himself, are with us. They are in the Bible and in the church. Long after this beautiful scene on the mountain the disciples remembered what God said, "Listen to Jesus."

The way to remember all the beauty God has for us is to stay close to Jesus and hear him.

When It Is Hard
to Be Good

Have you ever tried to work a yo-yo? It looks so easy when you see someone else do it. They just flip it down and up it comes again. Or they'll flip it down and let it "sleep" at the end of the string, then with a simple pull bring it right back up. Then I try it. First it is hard to wind up the string. *(Experiment with the toy.)* Then it wants to stay down. Or it just hangs there and spins around. It is surely hard to be good at it.

But you and I have seen boys and girls who can do this really fine, so we know that despite all the things that so easily go wrong, it is possible to be good.

When the disciples first followed Jesus they thought that being good was going to be easy. Soon they found that many

Scripture: Mark 9:9-13

Object: *a yo-yo*

---

things had to be overcome. Jesus knew that sometimes even the best people are hurt by evil, and that he was going to have to die. Of course, that didn't stop him because he knew he'd rise again; but he knew it would be hard.

I'm sure you have found that, too. Sometimes you really want to be good, and it looks so easy for other boys and girls, but when you try, things go wrong. You think, "I'm going to help mom." But, oh, the job she gives you to do makes you so tired, and it seems so long.

We all know, it is just plain hard to be good.

We know it, Jesus knows it. But that didn't stop him and it shouldn't stop us. We know being good is worth all the effort it takes.

Go to God
in Prayer

I wonder if you can remember back before you could tie your own shoelaces. Maybe some of you are still learning. But if you do remember, shoes were one of the biggest problems. Sometimes they would go on the wrong feet. Once they were on, the laces had to be tied or the strap buckled, and that was hard to do. The fact was that even after you could put all your own clothes on, there were always shoes yet to handle.

Of course, we had ways of handling it. Sometimes we just didn't put shoes on, but parents fuss about that. Sometimes we did as best we could, but left them untied. That worked pretty well. But to do it right there was only one way, we went to mom or dad and said, "I can't get this." They would then do the tying and slowly teach us to do it a little bit

Scripture: Mark 9:14-29

Object: *a child's shoe (preferably one with shoestrings)*

---

better. Yes, when we can't do something, it is best to turn to someone who can.

The man in our lesson today is someone who had tried to help his sick boy for many years, but the boy hadn't gotten better. Now he knew he needed help. He found that many people who thought they understood were no help so he came to Jesus. Jesus told the man, and his disciples, that the only real help is to ask God in prayer. So Jesus prayed, and the boy was healed.

Yes, girls and boys, there are many things we can do ourselves, but a wise Christian knows that over and over again there is only one best way to handle a problem; that is to pray to God. We believe in God and we know that when we pray he helps us. Then we believe in him even more.

Helping Others Understand

One day Jesus was explaining to his disciples what it meant to be great according to God. He told them about how sometimes God's servants had to be quiet when they felt like arguing. He told them how God's servants sometimes had to allow other people to go in front of them, like in line, or let them use things first. He told them God's servants sometimes wouldn't get a lot of attention from everybody but would work well and do a good job even if people did not notice them. He told them that he himself would allow himself to be killed in order to be helpful and save the world, although he knew he would rise again.

But you know adults don't always understand what it is to be meek and take things quietly and patiently. And the disciples just didn't understand what he was saying. Jesus

Scripture: Mark 9:30-37

Object: *a child*

---

needed something to show them how to be his disciples. You know what he decided would show what he meant? He looked around him and found a child. *(Pick out a child here.)* He stood the child right in the middle of the men and women, very near to him. He put his arm around the child so he or she would feel good even though everyone was looking. Then he said, "You should try to be as gentle and quiet as this child is. You should trust God like this child trusts me. You should be ready to follow just like this child."

You see, Jesus said that you boys and girls can help people know what it is to be a Christian by being loving, trusting, humble and good. Jesus thinks a lot of you. He says children are very important. You, more than anyone, can help people understand what it means to be a servant of God.

Who
Belongs?

Do you see this? It tells you I belong to a group. All the people who sent for one, or asked for it, got one; and now I'm a member, too. Everybody has probably gotten a chance to join something like this. All it takes is some money or a good friend to get you in.

Some boys and girls have their own club, maybe a secret club. Maybe some of you belong to a club that has a secret knock or password to get you in. It is fun to belong to something, to know that you are in with others in a good thing.

The disciples knew they belonged to an important group. They belonged to Jesus. They really felt good about it. But they didn't have a badge or a hat to tell them they belonged,

Scripture: Mark 9:38-50

Object: *identifying badge or hat, ring, etc., from cereal box club or local fast food chain*

---

just like today it isn't necessary to have Christians wear a sign which says, "I am a Christian." But they did ask Jesus how you can tell a Christian if he doesn't have a badge.

Jesus said, "It isn't what you wear that shows you are a Christian, it's what you *do*." Like, if someone is thirsty and you get him a drink, that shows you are one of Jesus' people. If you see that something is bad for you and you stop doing it, that shows you belong. In fact, anything that helps make things good and happy for those who are around you is just the kind of thing that shows you belong to Jesus.

Not what you wear, but what little things you do shows who belongs to Jesus.

Marriage
Is Sharing

I have brought today two containers of colored water. They are beautiful all by themselves, clear and fine. This one is red. This one is blue. But both Mr. Red and Miss Blue see this larger container and think, "Ah, that is a bigger place where we could be with each other and share everything." *(Pour both into the larger container.)* Oh, what happened? Yes, the color seemed to change.

Actually, if you talked to a scientist he would tell you that there are still red molecules and blue molecules in there, but in sharing the same place they have become one new color when you look at it.

The reason I showed you this is because today I want to talk about marriage. If you've ever been to a wedding, you saw two people, a man and a woman *(lift the empty containers)* agree to share their lives so that both would have a

Scripture: Mark 10:6-9

Object: *two clear containers of water, one blue, one red. Use food coloring. When mixed they are to produce a violet. (One can use blue and yellow to make green.) They are to be mixed in the course of the talk in a larger clear container. A little experimentation will produce the right hues.*

---

larger life, a fuller life *(indicate the larger container)*. They really both remained who they were, your aunt or uncle, your sister or brother. But they agreed to share their lives and everything with another so that now when they come to visit they are together. When you get a birthday card they both sign it. God has joined them and even though they are still themselves, together they are something new and more beautiful than when they were not joined in marriage.

This is the way your parents share life, too. They are two persons whom you love, but in a special way they share. You love them together and they love you, together. That's the way God made man and woman, to be able to be something special when they share their lives. Marriage is sharing. Isn't it beautiful?

Welcome
Without Price

If you go to the movies, first you must have a ticket. If you go on a ride at a fair, you must have a ticket. If you want something at a store, first you must pay for it. That's the way it is all over in our world. It seems that before you get anything you have to give something.

Sometimes it is not what you give, but who you are that seems to count. Did you ever feel that it was only bigger people or older girls and boys that get to do things? Sometimes it seems as if everything you want to do, someone says, "Wait until you're older," or "Wait until you grow up more, then you can do that."

I suppose there are some things that wouldn't be safe for you, or good for you until you're older; and people do need to be paid for things you get. However, I know one very

Scripture: Mark 10:13-16

Object: *strip of tickets*

---

important and wonderful thing you can get to with no special price. That is the kingdom of God. Jesus tells us that everyone is welcome no matter who they are.

Once when little children wanted to see Jesus the disciples thought, "Oh, they ought to be bigger or be something special to get to see Jesus." But Jesus saw them trying to keep the little children away and he told them that everyone was welcome to be close to him and close to God.

Just to show them, he gathered the children all around him and hugged them. They sat on his lap and he put his hands on each one to bless them. How good it is to know that Jesus wants us to be close like that. One thing we know about Jesus is he will always welcome us no matter who we are.

Life Comes
to You

Butterflies are beautiful. But have you ever tried to get close to one? If you are in a field with butterflies and try to walk up to see it close, it always flies away. If you grab at one to catch it, again, it flies away. The only way to see a butterfly up close is to sit quietly in the field and wait. Soon, if you are quiet, a butterfly may come close and maybe sit right near you. If you grab, it flies; if you wait, it comes.

So it is with trusting and knowing God. Like a beautiful butterfly, Jesus tells us that God gladly comes to us. Some people think they can get close to God by working very hard. They say, "If I follow the laws then God will like me,"

Scripture: Mark 10:17-27 (28-30)

Object: *a butterfly (can be made out of cardboard or a picture)*

---

or "If I say the right things then God will be close to me." They discover that the more they think about what they do or what they have the less they really think about God. That's like grabbing for the butterfly. It doesn't work. They find it is harder just to believe that God loves them.

The fact is that trusting and knowing God is something that happens not because we do anything but because God comes to us. If it were up to us, we'd chase and work and try, and we'd get nowhere. But God always loves and comes to us with his life. Now, isn't that beautiful?

It's Hard
to Follow

(Play a game of Simon Says where the leader does various things which "Simon says" to do and then leave out the "Simon says" which direction is not to be followed. A few brief rounds of this will be enjoyable and not disruptive even for a church service.)

Whew, that's hard to follow sometimes, isn't it? You think you can do it. You try to listen very hard. Then whoops, you miss anyway.

There are many people who start to follow Jesus. They are pretty sure they can do anything that's necessary. Well, they think that means praying ... "I can do that." It means being good to my friends and neighbors ... "I can do that." It means going to church and Sunday school and that's easy. Oh yes, and being helpful around the house doing the little things your parents need done. Now that's a bit harder, but it's okay, too.

You see, if you just listen to what promises not to change what you are doing already, then there is no problem.

Scripture: Mark 10:32-34

Object: *the game "Simon Says"*

What happened was that Jesus told his disciples what else he was going to do. He said he was going to a place, Jerusalem, where no one would like him, in order to help those people. He said he was going to love people who would hurt him. Even unfriendly and mean people would be loved so much that he would even die for them.

We read that when he started to go, the people who had followed him were afraid. It is hard to follow Jesus when everyone else isn't. It's hard to follow when nobody notices how well you're doing. It's hard to follow when nobody says "Thank you for helping me." Even though you try to follow you can't always do it.

But you know what? His disciples followed him anyway. They saw him get hurt, but they saw God raise him again. So they kept following Jesus just as we do. Sure sometimes it's hard to follow. But that also means that we are always with him. Nothing could be better than that.

Who Gets
the Prize?

Now isn't that something glorious? I imagine the team worked hard to get this. They practiced, ate the right things, learned to handle the ball and plays. They studied and worked. They won many games and at the end they won the prize. I'd bet they were proud and happy.

It is wonderful to win the prize. After all, few people manage to do that. Not everybody sticks to the training long enough or wins enough. Only very few are winners. I'm not surprised that when James and John were with Jesus they thought about winning the prize. They thought it would be great. They knew Jesus didn't give trophies. The prize for Christians is to be very close to God, to be in his kingdom for ever.

Naturally, they thought like in everything else, the prize is

Scripture: Mark 10:35-45

Object: *a trophy (the bigger the better)*

---

given to whoever works the hardest. Then everyone applauds with lots of congratulations. But that's not the way to be close to Jesus or to God. Jesus didn't look for applause. He didn't look for congratulations. He gave his life.

Besides this, none of us can earn the prize of being close to God. God chooses us. Being close to God isn't kept just for one or two people, or for just a few. It is given to everyone who trusts God and loves and serves him. You don't have to think prizes are just for others. It is for all God's servants.

I'm sure that at first James and John were disappointed they weren't special. But they found out that being with all of God's people means being close to God. That is the finest prize anyone can have.

A Support
Only When Needed

You boys and girls have seen people use one of these from time to time. It is a crutch. It is used when you need support for a foot, or ankle, or leg. If a bone is broken or a muscle is sprained you put this or a pair of them in your hand to walk with, in place of the leg that is hurt or weak.

Of course, once the leg is better or stronger, a person is very glad to put the crutch away and walk by himself or herself. It would be just as silly and wrong to use a crutch when you are able to walk all right, as it would be not to use a crutch when you really need it.

The man in our story today really needed Jesus. He was blind and so he couldn't do the things God wants us to do. He wanted to help, but he couldn't. He wanted to work, but not seeing kept him from doing things. He knew he needed Jesus to lean on. He called out to Jesus for help. Even though

Scripture: Mark 10:46-52

Object: *a crutch*

---

people told him that Jesus was too busy he kept calling because he knew he needed Jesus.

We know Jesus was glad to hear him call. He stopped everyone to help the man. It is just as we find out; if we really need help Jesus will listen. There are times when you are sick, or when you have something that is very hard to do that you must call on Jesus. Maybe you would ask help for someone you really care about. If we call, he listens, and helps.

Then when we are over our trouble, even though we still talk to Jesus in prayer, we have to get up and follow him. That is, just like the man who had his blindness healed we also are to start up again to do the things we should do. A crutch is for when you are weak. When God makes you strong then the thing to do is to follow Jesus, helping others just as he did for you.

Hail to
the King

When Jesus rode into Jerusalem, if you didn't know who he was you would think he was an ordinary person. He didn't dress any differently than he ever did. He rode like a king, however, and everyone right away knew that Jesus was a king.

But what is he king over? He has no land to rule. He has no government to control. He has no taxes paid to him. He has no army or navy. But he was a king all right. A different kind of king. A king wise and wonderful. The king of important things. He wears many crowns.

(*Hold up one crown.*) He is King over the Church. All the people who love God follow Jesus. Boys and girls, mothers and fathers, everyone who is among God's people praise him. Hail to the King of the Church!

(*Hold up another crown.*) He is King of Love. Jesus shows us how to love when he goes through his life sharing and

Object: *four crowns made of gold paper*

---

giving. Most of all, when he goes to the cross and even dies for us we see how to love. No one has so much love as he. Hail to the King of Love!

(Hold up another crown.) He is King of Peace. When his kind of love comes into our lives, when people love as he loves, then we have peace with one another. He is the maker of all peace. Hail to the King of Peace!

(Hold up the fourth crown.) He is King of Life. He rules over the whole world, the whole universe. From strongest mountains to the deepest sea, he is king. Wherever we see he is the king. Hail to the King of Life!

Girls and boys, more than all this, the most important thing we can say is "He is *my* king." You and I know that Jesus comes to rule for us. Hail to my king! Hail to King Jesus!

He Comes
to Save

Once there was a boy who was visiting his grandfather. His father said, "You have your good clothes on today. You cannot climb in the trees in the orchard out back."

Well the day wore on and as the adults talked the boy wandered out to the trees. My they looked good. Just one leg over a branch wouldn't hurt. Soon another was up. Before long he was up in the tree.... But, oh, he was high. Too high. The ground was so far away... and his pants got caught. He was doing what he wasn't supposed to do and he was stuck without help.

Then he heard the door of the house close. It was dad, and his dad called his name. How do you think he felt? Should he answer? He would get scolded... but he needed help. Finally he called, "Here I am."

Scripture: Mark 11:12-14, 20-26

Object: *a tree branch*

Sure enough, dad said, "Why are you in that tree?" and he was angry. It was terrible, but it was wonderful. Soon dad was up there giving him his hand, telling him where to put his foot. Before long he was on the ground and safe. He couldn't have been saved if he hadn't been ready to be scolded.

You see, boys and girls, God knows what is good for us. He tells us what it is good to do and what is not good. When we do things wrong and God comes, we feel guilty. But Jesus tells us to pray and ask God for help. Sure we feel foolish, but God knows we need him. So when he comes We're both scared, and glad. Even though we feel bad because of what we've done the important thing to know about God's coming is this: God comes to save us.

Someone's Coming

(Ring bell) What does it mean? . . . Someone's coming. . . . Who could it be?

(Ring bell) The house is a mess. Toys are all over the place. Our lives are a mess. Sins are all over the place. We try to straighten them out. Put them on the shelf. They don't all fit and they are still showing. Put them in a closet. You can't hide them, the door won't shut. Sins are so easily seen.

(Ring bell) Someone's coming. Maybe he has something for me. Maybe he's offering something good. Maybe he doesn't care what I look like . . . maybe he does care. Can I take what he brings?

Scripture: Mark 11:15-19

Object: *a doorbell (electric bells are easily connected with a 9-volt battery)*

(Ring bell) Someone's coming. Maybe he has come to help me straighten things out! Then it's okay to let him in as long as I am found trying to get things cleaned up. Maybe he has come to remove the sins with me.

(Ring bell) Someone's coming. It is Jesus. When he comes he does clean up and remove my sins. Jesus comes to take away what's wrong and put things right. He has a new way, a better way, to live.

(Ring bell) Someone's coming. Welcome Jesus! He has come to make everything right again.

What God Expects

I need someone to check out this ball. Would you like to look this over for me and tell me if it's okay? What do you expect of a ball? Of course, you do expect that it will bounce. If you didn't get to bounce a ball that would be a sorry state of things. And what we expect it does do, it bounces.

Now what if I had this fine ball, which is made to bounce well, and said, "It is so pretty, I think I will put it on the shelf where I can see it." So I put it there and dust it off every day. Then I bring my friends in to see it and show them this wonderful ball. What a waste that would be! A good ball, just sitting there. Boys and girls could be having a wonderful time with it. I suppose people would say that I must have no idea what such things are for. It would be sad.

You know, that is how God must feel. He made us to live

Scripture: Mark 12:1-9

Object: *a ball (which anyone would bounce)*

---

in his world. He made us to work for good and to return our good things to God. We are able to love others and be helpful. We are able to share that others will be happier and be taken care of. And so often we don't do those things at all.

God even sent Jesus to show us how to love and to give. Jesus gave so much that he gave us his life, but still we forget to return our blessings to God. Yes, we even forget Jesus. How sad that is; what a waste of our good things to put them to wrong use or not to use them at all.

God has made us to love and to honor Jesus. Doing that is the only way we can be all that God has made us to be. Loving and honoring Jesus by doing what he made us to do is what God expects.

What We Are Made For

It's that time of year. Already you girls and boys have seen the older people out in the garden doing many things. Maybe, if you were lucky, you got to go out to help. You might have turned the ground, or smoothed it, or planted, or kept down the weeds. Whatever you did, you found out that each tool has its own special purpose.

Now if you wanted to dig a hole, these clippers wouldn't really be very helpful. You would have to use the spade. But if you wanted to cut the weeds, the spade would be very awkward. For that the hoe is best. Of course the clippers are for trimming the plants. Each tool is made for certain things and we do well to know how to use and how to keep them.

Scripture: Mark 12:13-17

Object: *several garden tools (spade, hoe, rake, clippers)*

In our lives there are different things too. God has given us different skills and talents and they are to be used for different things. Digging can be for gardening, or for playing in the sand. Our arms can be used to lift packages for others. Our heads can think for many things. Our feet can bring us places. But our heart, that is our first love and our highest trust, that belongs only to God. The things we do, they may be great or small, but our loyalty goes first to God.

You know we have a wonderful country to support and to work for. We have a country and a city which needs our help. We are supposed to work for our families and our neighbors. But first, boys and girls, we are made for God.

Send Your
Roots Deep

You know, we only see half of every tree. We see the trunk, the branches and the leaves. We admire the shade of a tree and listen to the sound of the wind as it goes through. Sometimes we climb in larger trees and look down at the ground. But that is only half of the tree.

The other half is under the ground. That is the roots. Before a tree grows very much above the ground it sends out roots as deep as it can into the soil. They are there for many reasons. One is to get food and water from the earth for the tree to live on each day. In the winter the tree sends its juices deep down into the roots to stay safe until spring comes. That preserves the life of the tree. Yet another reason for roots is to keep the tree steady. When winds blow and rains come it is the roots which hold tight in the ground to keep the tree standing up the way it should. As you can

Scripture: Mark 12:28-34

Object: *small tree seedlings (Prepare by digging up and washing soil from roots. Keep roots in water to preserve freshness.)*

---

see, without deep and wide roots the tree would be lost.

This lesson today talks about the roots we have for our Christian life. Like the branches, we see the things Christians do, the way they act in life, but often we don't see the roots that feed that life and keep it steady. "You shall love the Lord your God, with all the strength you have" is one of those roots, and "You shall love your neighbor as yourself" is another.

You know, we see Christians gather at church and sing, read the Bible, help each other, and so forth. But what you don't see is the deep love that is the root of it all. Anyone who has this love is fed well, is safe, and is steady in hard times, just as these roots keep the tree. Jesus tells us to send our roots deep into the love of God.

Covering
Up Sin

I hope I didn't scare anyone too badly. *(Show mask, holding it in your hand.)* Ooh, isn't that ugly? It's sort of fun to have a mask like this, but no one wants that ugliness around for long. . . . I think I'll make it beautiful. *(Cover mask with the white cloth and hold the flower on it.)* There, now that face is all beautiful.

Oh, no, it isn't. It may be all covered up, but you and I know that is just the outside. Inside that mask is just as ugly as ever. It doesn't change the inside if we make the outside look good.

Think of a boy named Oscar. Let's say Oscar thinks mean thoughts about another boy at school named Sam. One day

Scripture: Mark 12:38-40

Object: *ugly Halloween mask, white cloth and flower*

---

when no one else is looking Oscar trips Sam so he falls down and tears his pants. Oscar then looks real nice and tells everyone that Sam slipped on a pebble. He makes it look good. Maybe everyone believes him, he covered it up, but inside Oscar is just as mean as ever. Sometimes you can cover up your sins, but that doesn't change how ugly it is inside.

We Christians know that it is Jesus who only is really able to change ugly sin into something better. The only thing we can do ourselves is to change what shows. Jesus comes into our lives and truly makes us good. With Jesus we become good inside, and that shows on the outside, too.

Using the
Things We Have

I'd like everyone today to get a treat and I'll need some people to give them out. *(Select children, including Tony, and tell them to give the candies to everyone. Everyone will soon notice Tony.)*

Thank you. I wonder if you noticed what Tony did? I've got to tell you that Tony is always glad to share, but I asked him not to so that we could talk about it. That surely looked funny to seem to be so selfish when others were sharing.

You see, boys and girls, the candies can either make everyone happy or they can be just for ourselves and make only a few happy. It isn't the candy that decides whether to share or to be selfish. It is we who decide that.

Scripture: Mark 12:41-44

Object: *several bowls or bags of candy. Several children are asked to help distribute candies so everyone can get one. However, one child has been instructed before-hand to take his (her) candies to one side and to start eating them. Let's call that child Tony.*

It is that way with everything we have from God. Toys, balls, even the songs we can sing. We can keep them only for ourselves, which may seem to make us happy. But God has better plans. He hopes that we use our things to make others happy as well. The money we have can be used just for ourselves or we can give it also for God and others. The time we have can be kept for just us, or we can use it to be helpful. Jesus tells us that the very best way to use what we have is to use it for the things God wants done. Even little things are very great when they are used well, when they are used for God.

God Makes
It Right

I'm going to do an arithmetic problem. You can think along with me. *(Put on board 2+2=)* Now let's see. Ah, I know it *(put down 3)*. Hmm, that's not very good.

However, I am fortunate. I have a good teacher who wants to help me, just like I have a good God who wants to help. A good teacher won't let that answer be that way. *(Erase the 3.)* Now what do I do? Do I say, "Look it may not be a good answer, but at least it was an answer, and now you've wiped it out?" No, because a good teacher is only satisfied with the best I can do. I should be glad the wrong answers are put away.

So, just as God forgives my sins, that old wrong answer is gone, wiped out. Now, of course, I don't just sit down. I

Scripture: Mark 13:1-13

Object: *a chalkboard or large pad to write on*

---

have to keep answering and changing until I come up with *(write 4)* the right answer. Only then can I be satisfied.

Girls and boys, in many ways our world is coming up with the wrong answers to life. We do things bad or wrong; we treat each other wrong; we need correction. God is not any more happy with this than we are. Just as we erased the "3," some things have to be destroyed when they are wrong. We have to be put to a test. This is not just to destroy but in order to make room for the right answers, for God's way.

God has promised that we will not have to live with wrong forever. He tells us he will remove the things that are bad so that, at the end, he can save those who stay close to him. The world may be wrong sometimes, but God will make it right again. That's a good thing to know.

Knowing the End
of the Story

This is a special kind of storybook. I imagine everyone of you girls and boys know every story in it. They are wonderful and good stories. Do you know what makes them so much fun? You know exactly how they will turn out.

You can be sad when Cinderella sees her sister go off to the ball at the palace because you know that she also will go to the dance. You can be excited when the clock begins to strike midnight because the prince will find the glass slipper and marry her.

When Goldilocks falls asleep in the middle bed and the bears come home to find their porridge eaten, you can hear them come upstairs because Goldilocks will escape safely. Or when Rumpelstiltskin hears the princess give all the wrong names, you know that the last name will be right and her child will be saved. You know the end of the story.

Scripture: Mark 13:24-31

Object: *Mother Goose storybook*

Christians feel the same way about life. Some days are fine and some days are not so good. Maybe something sad happens, or something glad. But for Christians every day can be great because you and I know how it will all turn out in the end. We know that no matter what happens in the meantime, Jesus is coming again to be sure that everything will be all right.

That means we can get excited about living. We can go through tough times and good times and still do the best job we can because we know that at the end of time God will gather all of his own people together. Then we will be close to God, and to each other, for ever. Yes, knowing the end of the story makes the whole of life that much more grand.

An Eye on
What Is Ahead

Did you ever wonder why, whenever you see a picture of a captain of a sailing ship he is carrying a spyglass? You see him on the bridge or on deck first checking things around him and then looking out far ahead. There is a good reason for that. Wherever you are, and especially when you are on the water in the ocean, you must not only know about what is close but you must also know where you are going. You can't steer right unless you can tell what is out ahead.

That is why we have headlights on our cars, too. The driver must see out in front in order to steer the car correctly. It helps to know both where you are and where you are going.

Scripture: Mark 13:33-37

Object: *a spyglass or binoculars*

That is the way Christians live, too. Surely we know the things which are going on around us, but we are also looking ahead. Jesus tells us that one day God is going to come to find out how we are doing and to set everything right. He even tells us what things God will be looking for, like how we are using what we own, how we are helping each other, and how much we are loving.

Yes, we are headed toward a life which will always be with God. We keep an eye on that time because it tells us what we should be and do that is good today.

A Promise
to Remember

When you want to remember something very important, how do you do it? Maybe you ask someone to remind you. Some people put a note in their pocket. One way is to put a string on your finger like this. Then whenever you look at it you know there is something you are not supposed to forget.

Today we have something important to remember. We remember that Jesus, who came to die for us, has promised to continue to work, doing God's will, in order to save us. That is really wonderful. Since he rose from the dead, our Lord Jesus will always be with us so that we can be children of God.

Just think, if we are ever afraid we can remember Jesus

Scripture: Mark 14:12-26

Object: *a string to tie on one's finger*

---

and the way he is near us. Or if we want to talk to God we can remember how he has made us children of God. If something seems wrong; we know that Jesus is working with us to make it right again. If we start to worry about something we can remember that he has saved us. And if we have done something bad, we know Jesus can bring us back to God.

I suppose to remember this we could tie a string on our finger, but Jesus had a better way. He gave us a very special meal with bread and wine. Whenever we eat and drink this bread and wine we remember his promise to be with us and to save us. It is a promise to remember.

How You
Look at It

Have you ever looked at a piece of cardboard? If you hold it one way *(face edge to the group),* on its side, a piece of cardboard is thin, long and narrow. Really, seen that way you would wonder that anyone ever used a cardboard.

If you turn the cardboard *(turn cardboard)* and see it from the front or back, it is broad and wide. Seen this way you know that people can paint on it, or make a poster to give a fine message, or make a picture. It is how you look at it that makes the difference.

Today we are looking at the time when Jesus died on a cross. Really, some people look at the cross and see only a terrible thing. Of course, it was terrible, it was hard and painful for Jesus. It is sad to know someone is dying, and

Scripture: Mark 15:33-39

Object: *stiff piece of cardboard or posterboard*

---

especially someone as good as Jesus. But that is the narrow way to see this. That is like looking at the edge of the cardboard.

Jesus allowed this to happen to him so that many people would be saved from sin. He knew he would die and he knew he would rise again on Easter. He didn't see only a narrow thing *(show cardboard sideways)* but he saw the broad and beautiful side of it *(turn cardboard)*. Because of Jesus' death we all are brought closer to God. It is truly amazing that all that good can come from Jesus dying on a cross. But it is so. It is all in how you look at it.

That is why today we are not sad, instead we give praise and thanks to God for sending Jesus to us. He has saved us.

Power
to See

These are batteries. Batteries are interesting and curious things. Just to look at them you would think they are nothing but short cylinders. You might be told they are "live" batteries, or even that there is power in them, but you can't see that power or feel it. You can't touch a battery and tell whether it is alive or not.

Maybe you believe me that these batteries are live and maybe you don't. I have a way to show that they are live and are filled with power. I can take this tube *(take flashlight)* which looks so dead and put the batteries in it. . . . Ah, now that dead tube is bright. What was just a piece of metal and glass is now a fine thing to give light all around. We can see the life in the batteries by what they do. We know they are live batteries, filled with power.

Scripture: Mark 16:1-8

Object: *two flashlight batteries and a flashlight*

We Christians tell the world that Jesus is alive, and that he has great and saving power. Like the batteries, many people can't feel the life in Jesus. There is no way to show them the power of the living Jesus just by talking about it. Maybe they believe and maybe they don't.

But just as we put the batteries into the flashlight, Jesus comes into our lives. He gives us the power to live for him. He brightens our lives so that we can brighten the lives of others. By our living others can see the life of Jesus and his power in us. We know Jesus is alive because he is in us. Through us everyone can see that Jesus lives.

Boys and girls, you and I are the living proof that Jesus is alive today.